C000293987

NOTTINGHAM IN THE 1960S AND 70S

DOUGLAS WHITWORTH

The
History
Press

Drury Hill on a peaceful Sunday morning in 1964.

Dedication: To John Lock.

First published 2009

The History Press
The Mill, Brimscombe Port
Stroud, Gloucestershire, GL5 2QG
www.thehistorypress.co.uk

© Douglas Whitworth, 2009

The right of Douglas Whitworth to be identified as the Author of this
work has been asserted in accordance with the Copyrights, Designs and
Patents Act 1988.

British Library Cataloguing in Publication Data.
A catalogue record for this book is available from the British Library.

ISBN 978 0 7524 4887 9

Typesetting and origination by The History Press
Printed in Great Britain

CONTENTS

ACKNOWLEDGEMENTS

My very special thanks are due to John Lock, whose photographs form the basis of this book. He had the foresight to realise that many historic buildings of the city were in danger of demolition and began photographing those at risk. I also wish to thank the following for the loan of photographs:

David Amos, Leonard Brownlow, Central Photographic Services Ltd, Fox Photos Ltd, Alice Harby, Nottingham Evening Post, J.H. Price, Richard Shelton, William Smalley and Viva Imaging. The photographs of F.W. Stevenson are reproduced by kind permission of Martin Sentance.

I am also indebted to Dorothy Ritchie and the staff of the Local Studies Library for their expertise, and the following for their help:

Mike Astill, Edwin Baker, Stephen Best, Kevin Fear, Carolyn Maginnis, Roger Paulson, Alan Trease, Vera Tyers, Rick Wilde, and Andrew Wilson. I also wish to thank my wife Margaret for her invaluable help and support in the production of this book.

The illuminated Christmas tree in the Old Market Square in 1962, with the floodlit Council House in the background.

INTRODUCTION

It was in the 1960s that the citizens of Nottingham saw the greatest change in the face of the city in the twentieth century. In the previous decade, the city planners envisaged a dual carriageway which would encircle the centre of Nottingham, and they began by building a new highway from Castle Boulevard to Friar Lane. Many slum properties were demolished in the area around Walnut Tree Lane near the castle, but a number of historic buildings were also swept away in the construction of the new road – notably the Collin's Almshouses and St Nicholas' Rectory. The following decade saw the extension and widening of Maid Marian Way, but the outcry against the indiscriminate razing of a whole district halted the construction of the planned inner-ring road.

The increase in car ownership in the 1960s was the stimulus for the building of inner-city motorways in Britain, and it also led to the running down of the railways and, as a consequence, the axing of several lines in the county including the Great Central – a direct line from Nottingham to London. In 1965 a planning committee approved the sale of the Victoria Station for £740,000; the land was to be the site for a shopping centre and apartment blocks. In addition, the complex was intended to include a theatre, hotel, leisure centre and cinema, although none of these were constructed. With foresight the Grand Central line, with all its tunnels and bridges in place, could have been the north-to-south tramline of today.

The construction of the Broad Marsh Shopping Centre, which complemented the Victoria Centre, was equally contentious. Built mainly on undeveloped land, cleared of the notorious back-to-back houses, the building of the centre saw the needless destruction of the ancient Drury Hill. After less than forty years the shopping centre, criticised for its poor architecture, is scheduled to be demolished and rebuilt on an even larger scale.

The worst act of vandalism in this period, and perhaps of the century, was the demolition of the Black Boy Hotel in 1970. The hotel was bought by Littlewoods in 1961 with the intention of building a department store on the site and, despite a vigorous campaign to save the building, the wonderful rococo structure fell to the contractor's wrecking ball.

Not all was doom and gloom, however – the new Nottingham Playhouse, after years of debate, was finally built and opened in 1963. The theatre drew national acclaim for its design and for the standard of the performances given under the directorship of John Neville. The productions ranged from the intensely dramatic *Death of a Salesman* to the delightful *Boots with Strawberry Jam* and the irreverent *'Owd Yer Tight*. On one occasion John Neville took a group of his actors to the Goose Fair to give an al fresco show to an enthusiastic audience.

In 1969 the Theatre Royal, in danger of closing, was purchased by the city council and during the following decade was restored. The character of the Victorian theatre was retained but the auditorium was remodelled and the antiquated dressing rooms and backstage facilities were all rebuilt.

Two film galas held in Nottingham in 1960 raised the profile of the city – the first, at the Elite Cinema, was D.H. Lawrence's *Sons and Lovers*, filmed in the county; and the second, at the ABC Cinema, was Alan Sillitoe's *Saturday Night and Sunday Morning* which gave a realistic impression of life in a Nottingham inner suburb.

In 1963 the Beatles – then virtually unknown – played with other groups to a half-empty house in the Elizabethan Rooms of the Co-operative store on Upper Parliament Street. A year later their appearance at the Odeon Cinema was a sell-out and the cinema was surrounded by fans eager to see their idols. The group managed to avoid most of the crowd by emerging from the cinema after their performance into an alleyway leading to St James's Street.

In the late 1960s discussions were held by the city council concerning the housing conditions in St Ann's and the Meadows. Demolition of sub-standard houses was already taking place in Hyson Green, to be replaced by high-rise blocks of flats. These buildings survived for less than twenty years due to their poor construction and the social problems encountered by the tenants.

On 30 January 1970 the St Ann's redevelopment was officially launched, and throughout the decade both good and poor structures were indiscriminately knocked down. Although the first estimate of houses to be demolished was 3,000, the final figure was 10,000 out of a total of 11,500. The new dwellings proved to be characterless and the inhabitants missed the community spirit of the old streets with their corner shops, pubs and off-licences.

The early 1970s also saw the redevelopment of the Meadows, with a small number of the better-built houses being retained. As with St Ann's, the proliferation of pedestrian footways was confusing to both inhabitants and visitors and provided happy hunting grounds for criminals. Arkwright Street – the direct route from the city centre to Trent

A *Nottingham Evening Post* reporter typing his story from shorthand notes in 1961 – direct input into a computer was still fifteen years away.

Bridge, and lined with numerous interesting shops – was truncated and the old Burton Almshouses on London Road were pulled down.

The transfer of Boots from High Street and Jessops from King Street to the Victoria Shopping Centre in 1972 led to a major change in the shopping patterns of the citizens of Nottingham. Of the four remaining department stores in the city centre – the Nottingham Co-operative, Tobys, Pearsons and Debenhams – only the latter still exists but now intends to move from the Old Market Square to the new Broad Marsh Centre when it is built.

In 1973 pedestrianisation was introduced in Bridlesmith Gate and three years later a Zone and Collar scheme was initiated in the city in an endeavour to ease the traffic problems. Park & Ride facilities were also introduced along with dedicated bus lanes. Luxurious Lilac Leopard buses were brought into use, but all these measures failed and were eventually discontinued. Parking wardens were also seen for the first time on Nottingham's streets in 1964 – these are still with us, as are the re-introduced Park & Ride scheme and bus lanes. Trolley buses, which many passengers preferred to motor buses, were taken off the roads in 1966 following a civic send-off.

Nottingham's three main employers – Player's, Boots and Raleigh – had mixed fortunes in the 1960s and 70s. Public concern over the health risks of smoking were beginning to surface, but in 1970 Player's took the bold decision to build a brand new factory at Lenton, said to be the most modern in the world. The striking No.2 factory on Radford Boulevard was gradually phased out and sadly has now been demolished.

Boots also moved from their original base, when they closed their head office on Station Street in 1968 and transferred to their Beeston site. They were later to vacate all their warehouses on the Island Street site, ending an association with the area of over 100 years.

A quiet afternoon at the Victoria Railway Station in 1960.

In 1960 Tube Investments acquired control of the Raleigh Cycle Company – in the process handing over the British Cycle Corporation to the Raleigh management. With the merger, Raleigh began making Hercules, Sun and Phillips bicycles. The new company's great success was the Chopper, introduced in 1970 for the younger rider wanting an off-road machine. With the growing competition from Far Eastern manufacturers, Raleigh was increasingly dependent on cult classics such as the Chopper and the later BMX and Burner models.

Nottingham began staging an annual festival in 1970 with a wide-ranging programme of events throughout the city. The highlights were exhibitions, military band concerts, manned balloon races, a regatta, an international horse show and a spectacular firework display in Wollaton Park. In the Old Market Square events included a carnival procession, a miniature circus with trapeze artists and clowns, a medieval market and a funfair.

Concerts given during the festival ranged from the symphonic to the King's Singers and Semprini, whose recital at the Albert Hall in 1971 was given for old-age pensioners at a greatly reduced admission price. Unfortunately, the festival was under-funded and gradually the events became fewer until it finally closed in the early 1980s.

One feature of the festival which survived was the opening to the public of the cave system under the newly-built Broad Marsh Centre. These tours proved so popular that more caves have now been excavated and incorporated into the system.

Faced with the competition of television, these decades saw the final closure of most of the city's suburban cinemas, some being converted into bingo halls, others into supermarkets and the remainder facing demolition. The sole survivor in the suburbs is the Savoy Cinema, whilst the two remaining cinemas in the city centre in the late 1970s, the ABC and the Odeon, have now both closed.

During the visit of Queen Elizabeth II to Nottingham in 1977 as part of her Jubilee celebrations, the Queen performed the opening ceremony of the Queen's Medical Centre. The new hospital was then described as being the largest in the world, as anyone who has walked along its corridors can testify. Meanwhile, the old General Hospital on Park Row was being gradually run down.

A new landmark building was rising on the site of the old Empire Theatre at the end of the 1970s. A concert hall which had been on the drawing board since the end of the war was finally being constructed. Joined to the restored Theatre Royal, the Royal Concert Hall was to open in 1982 to wide acclaim.

Two local events occurred in the sporting field in 1975, which although not immediately significant, were, within the next few years, to become of international importance. The first was the arrival of Brian Clough as the manager of Nottingham Forest Football Club, who within three years of his appointment, and with the assistance of Peter Taylor, transformed the side from a Second Division team into champions of the First Division. In 1979 Nottingham Forest exceeded everyone's expectations and won the European Cup, and repeated the triumph the following year.

It was also in 1975 that Jayne Torvill and Christopher Dean began skating together at the Nottingham Ice Stadium, becoming regional ice champions the following year. The couple's four golden years were to come in the early 1980s, winning the European, World and Olympic titles to become great ambassadors for the City of Nottingham.

1

AROUND THE OLD MARKET SQUARE

The classical Council House, overlooking the formal layout of the Old Market Square in 1973. Events and exhibitions have always been held here – the travelling exhibition on the right is promoting careers in HM Submarines. To the left on the skyline are cranes above the almost completed Victoria Shopping Centre.

A warm summer's day in the Old Market Square in 1967. Office and shop workers are taking their lunch break and children on holiday from school are chasing pigeons. Private cars and motor and pedal cycles are parked in front of the Council House, and there is not a traffic warden in sight.

Elizabeth King's pork pie shop on Beastmarket Hill in 1960. Then already established for over a century, Mrs King's pork pies and sausages were celebrated for their quality. The building was pulled down in 1966 prior to the construction of Market Square House.

Below: Market Square House under construction in 1967. This office block, which replaced the 1920s Lloyds Bank building, unfortunately dominates the western end of the square.

Above: The Flying Horse Hotel, The Poultry in 1967. The inn, with a warren of oak-lined rooms, has a date of 1483 on the exterior which is debatable. In 1987 permission was given to convert the property into a shopping arcade, now known as the F.H. Mall.

Yates's Wine Lodge, Long Row West, in 1963. Known by locals simply as Yates's, the establishment also had the St James Bar and the luxurious Kings Hall Restaurant on the lower ground floor. The interior is one of the sights of Nottingham with its brilliant cut glass, gilt mirrors, statuettes and a huge tower clock. In front of Yates's are two traditional telephone boxes and a police box – the latter is believed to be one of only two now remaining in the country, which after restoration stands outside the police headquarters at Sherwood Lodge.

Replica Victorian gas lamps hanging outside the Imperial Hotel in St James's Street in 1963. Across the street is the Old Malt Cross Music Hall, at that time occupied by Chapman & Watson, wholesale drapers.

In 1997 the building was reconverted into a music hall, but despite initial success the venture failed and a café-bar with the old name now occupies the Victorian theatre.

Below: The reception at the Council House in 1967 to commemorate the Nottingham High School Founders Day. The youngest pupil, Andrew Selley, has his glass filled by the matron – Dorothy Chambers – watched by, from the left, Dr D.T. Whitcombe, the headmaster; S.G.N. Mitchell, chairman of the governors; and the Lord Mayor, Councillor Bernard Bateman. By tradition, the Lord Mayor receives 20s from the headmaster for the purchase of bread, cheese and ale and the pupil is given an old groat (see page 70).

A well–attended Salvation Army meeting in the Old Market Square in 1967. The Army's religious services have been a fixture here on summer Sunday evenings for over a century.

Members of the Ha Krishna sect on Long Row in 1973. They were familiar on the streets of Nottingham in those days, in their flowing robes, with their shaven heads, chanting and drumming.

A crowd heckling a soap-box orator in the Old Market Square in 1964. These regular open-air meetings were enjoyed by all who participated.

A Sunday afternoon in the Old Market Square in 1960 with a speaker having the attention of a good crowd. Listening on the left with his back to the camera is Bob Loughborough, an evangelist with the Open Air Mission, and sitting in the centre holding a bible is Mr Welsh, another regular speaker.

A Whitbread promotion for Dutch products in the Old Market Square in 1979. The young girl in national costume and clogs is preparing to hand out drinks, and the magnificent shire horses are suitably named Horsa and Hensa.

A fire at the Cavendish furniture store on Long Row West in 1966, attracting a crowd of onlookers. The proprietors of the shop would no doubt make a virtue of their misfortune by holding a fire damage sale after the restoration of the building. The premises are now apartments and a supermarket.

The West End Arcade, Long Row West, in 1967. The arcade was opened in 1927 as the West End Meat Market after the Shambles, behind the old Exchange, were closed, prior to the building of the Council House. To mark the occasion, the butchers gave a bullock to be divided among the poor.

The Old Market Square in a snowstorm in February 1979. The country was experiencing the longest cold spell for fifteen years and the month was the worst of the winter, with fierce blizzards blocking many roads in the county.

Equitable House, South Parade, in 1961. The building was designed by T.C. Howitt in 1935 and was intended to complement the Council House, and to give the public a feeling of trust in the institutions occupying the building. The people queuing at the bus stop and passers-by are all formally dressed, as was the fashion at that time.

Opposite below: A snowy scene on Long Row in the ferocious winter of 1979. Conditions in the country were dire and the government appointed Denis Howell as the Minister for Snow. At the end of February a thaw began and conditions quickly improved.

Below: Federation Chambers at the corner of South Parade and Wheeler Gate in 1960. The building then contained numerous offices with Barnetts, who were described as ladies costumiers, on the ground floor.

Above: The end of an era in 1966, as the last Nottingham trolley bus prepared to make its final trip. Carrying a number of VIPs, the trolley bus made the journey from King Street to Valley Road followed by a convoy of twenty cars. On its return to the Lower Parliament Street depot a chorus of *Auld Lang* Syne was sung!

The Black Boy Hotel, Long Row East, in 1968, the year before its closure. The destruction of this distinctive Watson Fothergill building to be replaced by a utilitarian Littlewoods store was probably the worst act of vandalism in Nottingham in the twentieth century.

The statue of Samuel Brunts, who died in 1711, on the façade of the Black Boy Hotel. The hotel was owned by the Brunts Charity which founded the Brunts School in Mansfield. When the hotel was pulled down in 1970, the statue was taken to Mansfield and placed in the grounds of the school, although with its left hand missing.

Below: A children's roundabout in the Old Market Square in 1973 during the Nottingham Festival. In its early years, the festival was very popular, with events in the square ranging from pop concerts to fashion shows as well as attractions throughout the city. Many citizens were disappointed when the festival was discontinued through lack of funding.

Christopher Dean 'on the beat' on Long Row in 1980. Both Christopher Dean and Jayne Torvill had full-time jobs at the beginning of their wonderful years of achievement – practising their ice-dance routines at the Nottingham Ice Stadium in the early hours of the morning. With financial assistance from the city council, they were able to leave Nottingham to obtain professional tuition. In the early years of the 1980s the couple enthralled the whole nation with their dazzling performances. When Christopher Dean was a policeman, constables were not encumbered by an armoury of weapons, deterrents and communications aids, relying on old-fashioned attributes – common sense, good humour, trust and, in today's terminology, a high profile.

2

NORTH AND EAST OF THE SQUARE

The Palais de Danse at the junction of King Edward Street and Lower Parliament Street in 1973. When opened in 1925 the interior was the height of fashion and was patronised by the aristocracy, including on one occasion by Edward, Prince of Wales. The 1970s, in contrast, was the decade of decadent music which by 1980 had run its course.

The Quadrant sign outside the County Hotel in Theatre Square. The elegant frontage of the hotel was to disappear in 1975 when the building was pulled down before the construction of the Royal Concert Hall.

Below: The Theatre Royal and the Gaumont Cinema in 1964. The Theatre Royal, owned by Moss Empires, was in danger of closing, but in 1969 the city council, with great foresight and public spirit, bought the old theatre and in the following decade began its restoration. The Gaumont Cinema in the background was to close in 1971, the victim of falling attendances. Originally a music hall, the cinema still possessed a gallery, or 'the Gods', from where the view was almost vertiginous.

The Empire Theatre in 1960, two years after its closure. In its heyday, popular entertainers would give twice-nightly shows here. All the great English comedians and dance bands appeared at the Empire and, beginning in the late 1940s, American singers and comedians drew full houses to the theatre. After its demolition, the site was used for the long-awaited Royal Concert Hall.

The construction of the Royal Concert Hall in 1976. The saga of the city's new concert hall began during the war when plans were drawn-up for a new civic centre between Shakespeare Street and Forest Road to include a 5,000-seater hall. These proposals were all shelved. The purchase of the Theatre Royal and the Empire Theatre in 1969 enabled the authorities to renovate the former and commence building a concert hall.

The Mechanics Cinema in 1963 when the attractions were *St George and the Seven Curses* with Basil Rathbone and Estelle Winwood, and *Woman Like Satan* starring Brigitte Bardot. The Mechanics had a long history in the Victorian and Edwardian eras as a lecture hall, with notable appearances from Charles Dickens who gave a number of readings here. The hall was never very successful as a cinema, with only restricted views of the screen from the side balconies.

Milton Street in 1965 when all the buildings on the right were already threatened with demolition before the building of the Victoria Shopping Centre. On the right is the Milton's Head Hotel, noted for its music hall acts and pop groups. After its closure, a new Milton's Head survived for a few years on Lower Parliament Street.

Opposite below: The demolition of the Mechanics Cinema in 1964, overshadowed by the Victoria Station clock tower and Victoria Hotel. After the site was cleared a new Mechanics was built with shops at street level, but the new building, named Birkbeck House, was to last for only forty years before it was pulled down and rebuilt.

The Victoria Railway Station in 1964, the year its fate was sealed. Older citizens of the city have fond memories of the station with its great atmosphere, which the Midland Station lacked. British Railways were already cutting back their services through Victoria Station and by 1967 all long-distance trains had ceased running on these lines.

An atmospheric Victoria Station in 1960. Two grimy pre-war locomotives in their last days before their journey to the scrap yard. The diesel locomotives of today may be cleaner but railway enthusiasts would travel miles to see a scene such as this.

Opposite above: St Stephen's Arch on Lower Parliament Street in 1964. This archway led to St Stephen's Church, which was pulled down in the late nineteenth century before the building of the Victoria Railway Station. When Charles Taylor's veterinary business then moved here, they brought the stone horse from their premises in Clumber Street and had it placed above the arch. After the building was demolished in 1968, the horse remained in private hands before being sold at an auction in 2001.

Opposite below: The construction of the Victoria Shopping Centre in 1970. The building of this centre and the Broad Marsh Centre changed the shopping habits of the citizens of Nottingham. The department stores around the Old Market Square either moved into one of the centres or eventually closed down, leaving Debenhams as the only surviving store, with its future now uncertain.

29

The clock tower of the old Victoria Railway Station in 1973, dwarfed by the Victoria Centre flats. For a few years it housed the Clock Tower Restaurant but the tower now stands empty – a sad reminder of a magnificent railway station.

Opposite above: Looking south from the Victoria Centre flats in 1973, over Huntingdon Street Bus Station, which was shortly to close. Local inhabitants will probably remember beginning their East Coast holidays here – travelling by either Trent or Barton coaches – or more mundanely taking a mystery trip to a nearby beauty spot.

Below: The view northwards from the roof of the Victoria Centre flats in 1973. In the left foreground is Watson Fothergill's Rose of England public house, overlooked by York House – then home to BBC Radio Nottingham. On the right is the unused land cleared of the Great Central railway tracks and turntable.

The city centre from the Victoria Centre flats in 1973. This view has not changed greatly, apart from the high-rise buildings which have since sprung up on Maid Marian Way and the demolition of the North Wilford Power Station, visible in the distance.

Billy Smart's Circus parade on Mansfield Road in 1968, on its way to the Forest. A clown balances on the roof of the loudspeaker van, followed by elephants with uniformed girls on their backs. Next would come lions, tigers, bears and camels, which are seldom seen in circuses today.

Opposite below: The flower and seed avenue in the Central Market in 1971. Lowes, Wicks, Priestley's and Robinson's were regular stallholders and provided riots of colour from springtime onwards. Saturday evening was the opportunity to buy produce at bargain prices, particularly meat, poultry and fish. After the closure of the market a residential and office complex was built on the site.

Below: The Duke of St Alban's, Sherwood Street North, in 1963, the year in which it closed. Reputed to be the smallest pub in Nottingham, it contained only one public room, and below it were two levels of caves where the beer was stored. After its closure, the pub reverted to being a private house.

The Central Market in 1970, renamed the Festival Market for the period of the first Nottingham Festival. By this time the market had become well-established, and when it was transferred to the Victoria Centre in 1972, the dismay felt by the citizens was equal to that experienced when the market moved from the Great Market Place in 1928.

The Old Corner Pin at the junction of Clumber Street and Upper Parliament Street in 1976. Beginning life as the George, by 1799 the inn had become the Horse and Groom, and was then renamed the Old Corner Pin in 1910. After closing in 1989, the building was gutted to become a Disney store leaving only the façade. After a period as Etams, the shop is now a branch of Miss Selfridge.

The Lion Hotel, Clumber Street, in 1968. In appearance a typical Victorian public house with a glazed tile front, the Lion began life as a famous coaching inn which extended to Long Row. Now an amusement arcade, the building still retains underground caves which were used for cock-fighting in the eighteenth century.

The Crystal Palace, Clumber Street, in 1968. A Victorian pub built in art nouveau style, it suffered a similar fate to the Old Corner Pin and the Lion Hotel, and closed when the street became more commercialised.

The Bodega, Pelham Street, in 1962. Built in 1902 on the site of the Durham Ox, it was noted for its fine ports and sherries. Today it is known as the Social, one of many bars in the centre of the city which provide entertainment.

Boots, High Street, in 1966. This was Jesse Boot's first department store, built in 1903 by A.N. Bromley in the art nouveau style which was to be repeated by Boots in many other English cities. With the advice of his wife Florence, Jesse Boot opened toiletry, stationery and leather goods departments as well as a café and a Book Lovers Library in the shop. By the time Boots moved to the Victoria Centre in 1972, the two latter facilities had been discontinued.

Below: The Exchange, or Burton's Arcade, Christmas 1961. Joseph Burton & Sons had built up a flourishing business from a shop on Smithy Row which opened in 1864. When the Council House was completed in 1929, Burtons took several outlets in the Exchange Arcade. The firm, along with its rival Skinner & Rook, were famed for their high-class produce, but at Christmas Burton's drew crowds simply to view the decorations. Burton's closed in 1983, unable to compete with new supermarkets opening around the city.

3

SOUTH AND WEST OF THE SQUARE

An aerial view of Lister Gate in 1960, with 'Lucky Corner', the junction of Broad Marsh and Carrington Street, in the right foreground. This was the area which had most of the high cash trade shops in Nottingham including British Home Stores, Woolworths, C & A, Modes and Marks & Spencer.

Lister Gate in 1960 before this junction with Castle Gate was redeveloped. In this block were a number of well-known businesses, including Dewhursts the butchers; Lennon Bros., tobacconists; and James Day, jewellers. Weavers, established in 1844, had a public bar and off-licence in Lister Gate, connecting with a smoke room in Castle Gate.

Looking down Albert Street from St Peter's Churchyard on a busy and rainy Saturday in 1960. Crowds of shoppers are crossing Church Street either to or from the multiple stores in the area. Everyone is conventionally dressed with long top coats, and many of the women are wearing head scarves.

St Peter's Church Walk in 1961. This passageway from St Peter's Gate to Low Pavement, lined on the right with Victorian buildings, was eventually closed when Marks & Spencer extended their store across Church Street.

Below: St Peter's Gate in 1960. On the left is the Flying Horse Hotel garage, built into a Georgian house. Both this building and the adjoining Eight Bells public house were shortly to be demolished. A West Bridgford bus is making the circuitous route into the Old Market Square.

Above: The sign above the entrance to the Eight Bells on St Peter's Gate. The name is a reference to the bells of St Peter's Church, one of the oldest churches in Nottingham. The pub itself is eighteenth century with a reputation for rowdiness, perhaps the reason it was chosen before its closure in 1960 for scenes in the film *Saturday Night and Sunday Morning.*

Wheeler Gate on a quiet Sunday morning in 1964. On the left is Gant's glove shop and Sisson & Parker, the city's leading bookshop. The spires of St Peter's and the High Pavement Unitarian Chapel are prominent beyond. Although Marks & Spencer had taken over Style & Mantle's shop at the corner of their building, they had not yet extended across Church Street.

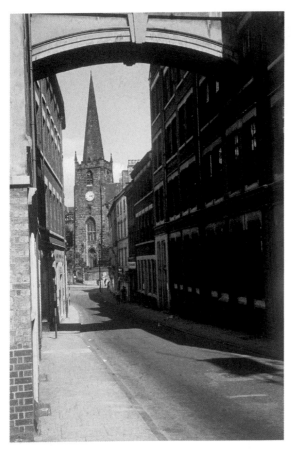

Hounds Gate towards St Peter's Church in 1964. One of the oldest streets in Nottingham, it led from the Norman castle to the English settlement around St Mary's Church. In Victorian times the street was lined with warehouses, including William Dixon's and James Snook's, whose bridge crossed the street.

Below: The Park Row Post Office in 1963. The upper windows of the building are relics of the old Houses of Parliament, which were destroyed by fire in 1834. The Gothic windows were rescued again and taken to the Black Boy in Market Street when this building was pulled down in 1965.

Above: Chapel Bar in 1966 when Maid Marian Way was being extended to this point. At the same time a pedestrian subway was constructed beneath the road, but this was to remain for only thirty years before being filled in again. Maid Marian Way did not enjoy the success forecast for it, receiving severe criticism for its ugliness and for slicing through an historic part of Nottingham. Recently, attempts have been made to soften the outline of the road by planting bushes and trees along the route.

Excavating the old town wall near Park Row, 1965. The wall, built in the thirteenth century, ran from The Ropewalk area, around the north of the town, to the present site of the National Ice Centre. After the excavations, any artefacts found were taken to the castle museum and the ground was refilled.

The Albert Hotel, Derby Road, 1968. A typical Victorian hotel with an array of chimneys, the Albert Hotel was popular with commercial travellers and with locals for functions. After its closure in 1970 the site was partly used for the building of the Strathdon Hotel.

Below: Nicholas McGegan rehearsing the Nottingham Harmonic Orchestra string section in the Albert Hall Institute in 1974. The orchestra was founded in 1941 and accompanied the Nottingham Harmonic Society Choir in many concerts, as well as giving purely orchestral concerts. The orchestra was disbanded in 1979 but the choir continues, having celebrated its 150th season in 2005.

The Nottingham Playhouse in 1964. The saga of the building of the new Playhouse began in 1958 when the city council agreed to its construction in East Circus Street, to be funded by money from the realisation of the Corporation Gas Undertaking. When the cost of the project escalated, the scheme was only saved by the casting vote of the Lord Mayor, Alderman Roland Green. The three artistic directors at the beginning of the first season in 1963 were Peter Ustinov, Frank Dunlop and John Neville, the latter being the stimulus to the success of the early years.

The Playhouse Bar & Restaurant in 1966. The city's reputation in the arts world was greatly enhanced by the success of the new Playhouse. On a warm summer's evening the terrace of the theatre takes on a continental atmosphere.

Above: Two nuns of the Order of the Sisters of Mercy tending plants in the Convent of Mercy garden, College Street, in 1965. The convent was designed by the eminent Victorian architect Augustus Pugin in 1844. Besides their devotional duties, the nuns also ran St Catherine's Grammar School which remained here until 1962, when it moved to Aspley and was renamed Loreto Grammar School. The Sisters of Mercy opened a nursing and residential home in the old school rooms in 1990, but with the decline in the number of residents and a lack of new entrants to the order, the home was closed in 1999. The building has since been converted into luxury apartments.

The Derby Road Baptist Church in 1966. Built in 1850, the church survived a major fire in 1906 before closing in 1960, when the congregation moved to the newly built Thomas Helwys Baptist Church in Lenton. After the church was demolished in 1971 this site was used for a modern office block.

4

AROUND THE CASTLE

Broad Marsh from the castle walls in 1968. On the left is St Nicholas Church, built after the previous church was destroyed during the Civil War by Parliamentarians. Beyond is Carrington Street, whose shops were due to be demolished prior to the building of the Broad Marsh Centre. In the distance is the spire of the High Pavement Unitarian Chapel and beyond is the tower of St Mary's Church.

A family eating lunch and feeding the ubiquitous pigeons in the castle grounds in 1966. Beyond are the eighteenth-century houses which, when restored, were to become until recently the home of the Museum of Costume and Textiles. The view towards the Council House was unspoilt by the high-rise buildings which were later to disfigure the city.

Geoffrey Trease at the launch of his book, *Nottingham – A Biography*, in the Long Gallery of Nottingham Castle in 1970. The Nottingham-born Trease, author of over 100 books, had just presented an autographed copy to the Lord Mayor, Councillor Oscar Watkinson.

Below: Geoffrey Trease, centre, talking to guests at the launch of his book on Nottingham, including, on the right, Professor Robert Leaney and his wife Elizabeth. Trease was a prolific writer of children's books, as well as histories and biographies. His first book, *Bows against the Barons*, was a bestseller – a realistic story of Robin Hood and his band of men.

Brewhouse Yard in 1961, when the houses were still inhabited. After renovation, this late seventeenth-century building was opened as the Brewhouse Yard Museum of Social History, now the Museum of Nottingham Life. On the left, in the distance, is Gibraltar House, once one of the many inns of Brewhouse Yard, and at the time beyond the town boundary.

The Trip to Jerusalem in 1961, reputed to be the oldest inn in England and, with its position, probably the alehouse of the castle. The inn, even with its questionable age, is one of the tourist attractions of the city, with its bars cut out of the rock face and underground caves.

Severn's, Castle Road, 1970, opened for the festival of that year. The building, part of a fifteenth-century merchant's house, was originally on Middle Pavement and was saved when the Broad Marsh Centre was planned. The timbers were taken apart and after being numbered were brought to Castle Road and re-assembled. Beyond in Hounds Gate, work is progressing on a modern office block replacing the Georgian houses that were ruthlessly destroyed (see pages 76 & 77).

The whale bone outside the Royal Children in Hounds Gate, a relic from the earlier inn which was pulled down in 1933. The name of the inn derives from the unfounded story that the children of Princess Anne, daughter of James II, were playmates of the innkeeper in 1688. The whale bone indicated that whale oil was sold in the inn for lighting lamps.

The restoration of Newdigate House, Castle Gate, in 1965. One of the most splendid houses in
Nottingham – its history is unique. Marshal Tallard, defeated in 1704 at the Battle of Blenheim, lived here
on parole for seven years. His stay had a lasting effect as he created a French garden behind the house
and began the cultivation of celery. By the beginning of the twentieth century the house was occupied
by a number of small businesses and it gradually deteriorated, until in the early 1960s the city council
considered opening a museum here. In 1964, however, the Nottingham and Notts. United Services Club
bought the property and began its restoration. At the same time a high-rise office block was built on the
site of a seventeenth-century house in the Dutch style adjoining Newdigate House.

The much-criticised Maid Marian Way from the roof of Newtown House in 1965. In the middle foreground is the well-restored Old Salutation Inn and beyond is St Nicholas Church, and it is clearly seen that many cars are using part of the roadway as a temporary car park.

Above: Maid Marian Way in 1965 before the road widening. Unfortunately, little thought was given by the planners to the impact the tall buildings would have on the area. Today, jaywalkers would not attempt to cross this road.

The grim underpass beneath Maid Marian Way and Friar Lane in 1968. Thirty years after this underpass was built, the tunnel has been filled in and street crossings have been restored. Youngsters appeared to be the only ones who derived any pleasure from the subway.

Above: The utilitarian People's College of Further Education, Castle Road, in 1960. The college was built on the site of St Nicholas Church School and destined to last for only half the time of its predecessor, due to be pulled down when the Broad Marsh Centre is redeveloped.

The Albany Hotel, Maid Marian Way, in 1971. During the building of the hotel, a tower crane and much of the scaffolding collapsed, fortunately with little human injury. A Green Shield shop on the left is advertising a sale, including shift dresses at 85p and garden chairs at £1.49.

Above: The Council House in 1968 apparently dwarfed by offices on Maid Marian Way. The building on the left, then occupied by British Telecom, has now been converted into the Park Plaza Hotel. In the foreground is a Wimpy Bar, at that time becoming popular with teenagers. The office block on the right is Loxley Court.

Postern Street towards Park Row in 1968. Spanning the street is the bridge from the General Hospital to the old Fever Wards. This was the second bridge over the street, the first being an elaborate copy of the Bridge of Sighs in Venice, but the benefactor, Sir Charles Seely, so disliked it that he had it demolished with only the two figures of saints being retained. The second bridge was pulled down in 1994 and the ironwork and figures were then sold to an architectural scrap dealer.

5

BROAD MARSH

Franks, newsagent, in Broad Marsh in 1969 – one of the last shops in the district before it too was demolished. The building was timber-framed and one of the few examples then remaining in the city.

A presentation to members of the Mayflower Trust outside the Sawyers Arms, Greyfriar Gate, in 1970. On the 350th anniversary of the *Mayflower*'s historic voyage to America, the Lord Mayor of Nottingham, Alderman W.G.E. Dyer, hands a cheque to Patricia Rasell and her mother Margaret, descendants of Captain Samuel Fuller, the doctor on board the vessel. The couple were making the journey by coach from Boston to Plymouth to replicate the original journey. Also in the group are Wendy George (Miss Great Britain) and Diana Wray (Miss Boston).

The Sawyers Arms, Greyfriar Gate, in 1969. This public house replaced an earlier pub which earned a reputation during the Second World War for brawls, particularly between American and Canadian service personnel. The new Sawyers Arms moved with the times and had a steak bar as well as the usual bars, but it finally closed in 1988.

Elephants from Roberts Brothers Circus trudging along Castle Boulevard in 1973, watched by eager families. After arriving at the Midland Railway yards, the procession of animals and vans proceeded to the Forest where the Big Top would be set up.

Lister Gate from Broad Marsh in 1966, when this was still the main route south from the centre of the city. On the left are the modernist shops of Woolworths and British Home Stores, with the spire of St Peter's Church and the dome of the Council House contrasting admirably in the distance. The only evidence remaining today of the old Broad Marsh is the street name on the corner of the building on the right.

Below: A surviving building in Broad Marsh in 1968, before suffering the fate of the whole district. The Victorian building was one of numerous lodging houses in the Broad and Narrow Marshes, when they were the most notorious districts in Nottingham.

Above: Narrow Marsh looking westward in 1970. Above the railway bridge is the redundant Weekday Cross signal box on the old Great Central line which closed in 1968. On the left is Malt Mill Lane which, with the arches beneath the viaduct, was to survive until the construction of the new tramline to Station Street.

The Lincoln Arms, Canal Street, 1969, shortly after its closure. With the demolition of the last of the nearby houses, the pub lost most of its trade and was forced to close. Kingston's in the unusual adjoining building were motorcycle dealers, shortly to move to new premises.

Above: The corner of Broad Marsh and Middle Marsh in 1968. Ron's hairdressers, originally Ward's, is clinging to life – as are several other small businesses on this corner.

Broad Marsh in 1968, showing some life due only to passengers leaving the nearby bus station. The area, which at one time was brimming with activity, was gradually dying – only to rise in another form.

Shirley's newsagent shop in Broad Marsh in 1968, bravely carrying on with its business. One of the posters on display outside the shop is for the *Daily Mirror*, which was publishing articles on English cities and on this day was featuring Nottingham and its great changes.

Below: On the left is John Player's original factory in Broad Marsh in 1968, the year it was demolished. Having opened a seed and fertiliser shop on Beastmarket Hill in 1862, John Player began selling loose tobacco and then cigarettes. In 1877 Player took over the long-established Broad Marsh tobacco factory of Joseph Wright and immediately began planning the growth of the business. Player commenced building three factories in Radford but died before their completion, leaving his two sons to continue the company's expansion.

John Lock posing by his Morris Minor Traveller on Drury Hill in 1968. The road, the old route south from Nottingham, had already been condemned, despite strong opposition from local civic bodies. The road, obviously only wide enough for one vehicle at a time, in the past would have been the scene of fierce arguments between carters and carriage drivers.

Below: The buildings on Drury Hill being demolished in 1971, although the route from Middle Pavement to Broad Marsh remains open. The old buildings of this street, were not great architecturally, but together with its steeply curving incline, made Drury Hill unique and it should have been preserved. Many old caves were uncovered during the demolition and have since become part of the system of caves opened beneath the Broad Marsh Centre.

Above: The bus station in Broad Marsh in 1968. This was intended to be a temporary measure only, but the station was to remain for over fifteen years. The Great Central viaduct, with its arches used for small businesses, has now been replaced by the Nottingham Express Transit line. Beyond is the High Pavement Unitarian Chapel, which after closing in 1980 was first used as the Lace Hall and now is the Pitcher and Piano bar.

The sign over a doorway in Narrow Marsh in 1964 advertises good lodgings for travellers. Double beds cost 6*d* and single beds were 3*d*. This lodging house was one of over forty which existed in Narrow Marsh in the nineteenth century.

The Loggerheads in Cliff Road in 1966, previously known as Red Lion Street. This is the only surviving pub from the many which were once in the Broad Marsh area. Legend has it that the Loggerheads was one of the haunts of the highwayman Dick Turpin.

Below: The Lace Market from London Road in 1969. In the foreground are the Plumptre Almshouses, built in 1959 to supplement the older building in Plumptre Square. The almshouses were founded by John de Plumptre in 1392 for two chaplains and thirteen aged widows, and were to remain in Plumptre Square until 1991 when the old building was closed and eventually converted into offices. The modern almshouses closed in 1998 and were later demolished. On the plateau above are the ancient Church of St Mary and the old warehouses of the Lace Market.

St John's School, Station Street, in 1970. This was built after the previous school and St John's Vicarage were demolished in 1892 before the viaduct for the Great Northern railway line was constructed. After the school closed in the 1930s the building was used by Boots as their personnel department until it was demolished in 1971. The building in the background is another Boots office block, built in 1968 and demolished in 2004 to be replaced by Jury's Hotel.

St Patrick's School in Plumptre Square in 1963, the year in which it closed. The school attached to St Patrick's Church was built in 1860 for the increasing population of Narrow Marsh. On the right in the background is the Nottingham Ice Stadium, an asset to the city since 1939 and now replaced by the National Ice Centre.

Collin Street in 1975, the year the Broad Marsh Shopping Centre was officially opened. The road – part of the city's inner-ring road – is as ugly as Maid Marian Way, with the faceless wall of the shopping centre on the left. Attempts have been made to change the image of the street, with little success. All these buildings are due for demolition before the new precinct is built. This road will then be closed, ending the practice of young motorists using this circuit as a racetrack.

6

THE LACE MARKET AND HOCKLEY

The Lace Market from the south in 1969. This was the period when many warehouses in the historic Lace Market were demolished without thought being given to the impact on the area. Fortunately, wise counsel prevailed and the district is now witnessing a renaissance.

The Nottingham High School Founders Day procession from St Mary's Church in 1964. The Lord Mayor, Councillor Bernard Bateman, and the headmaster, Dr. D.T. Witcombe, are led by the macebearer and followed by the Sheriff, Councillor Rex Rolling. The commemoration service, apart from the annual Goose Fair, is the most ancient ceremony still perpetuated in Nottingham, having commenced in 1513. The school was founded by Dame Agnes Mellers in honour of her husband, the bell-founder Richard Mellers. After the service a bread, cheese and ale reception is held at the Council House for the dignitaries (see page 13).

Garners Hill in 1979, one of the routes from the old town to the Meadows. In 1844 it was the scene of a tragedy when twelve people were killed during a panic at the execution of William Saville outside the Shire Hall.

After the destruction of the Black Boy Hotel, two of the stone lions from its roof were placed in the small park on Garners Hill. The park is now the site of the city's controversial new art gallery.

Above: Weekday Cross in 1968. This was the site of the old weekday market until 1800. From the middle of the nineteenth-century lace warehouses and factories were built throughout the area. The factory in the background was built for the yarn merchants, Holland & Webb. The white building on the left was the Barley Mow public house, which closed in 1950.

The wrecker's ball demolishing Yorkshire House at the corner of Warser Gate and Fletcher Gate in 1970. This was the period when the Lace Market was becoming run-down and buildings were demolished without thought for the future. After standing vacant for a number of years, the site has been used for apartments and retail outlets.

A Georgian house in Warser Gate in 1969, which unfortunately was not saved when the Philips Electrical Company moved out. The recent change to a largely residential district would have seen this building in the Lace Market preserved.

Below: An eighteenth-century town house at the corner of Pilcher Gate and St Mary's Gate in 1960. This Grade II listed building has a decorative central staircase and is one of the most important buildings of the period in the district. In the nineteenth century the house was converted into a lace finishing warehouse, when a semi-circular portico was removed. In the 1930s another drastic alteration was made when the two storey high windows were inserted in the frontage. In recent years the building has been allowed to deteriorate but there are now plans for its restoration. The adjoining Victorian building is also empty and in urgent need of renovation.

Above: The Windmill Inn in 1968, at the corner of Weekday Cross and Pilcher Gate, was once known as the Four Coffins and later as the Crown and Cushion. Pilcher Gate was named after the pilchers or furriers who lived in the street. The public house was demolished before the widening of Fletcher Gate in the early 1970s.

The Three Tuns, Warser Gate, 1968. The pub, which derives its name from the casks of beer or wine, was demolished at the same time as the Windmill Inn in Weekday Cross. The building on the right survived and now possesses a roof garden.

Above: The Cross Keys, Fletcher Gate, 1970 – a typical, well-preserved Victorian public house. The pub has always been noted for its talented musicians and entertainers. On the left is Byard Lane, where in the year of this photograph Paul Smith, the fashion designer, opened his first shop.

Bottle Lane in 1970 – one of the many narrow streets which existed in Nottingham in the past. This lane led from Bridlesmith Gate to the old English Borough around St Mary's Church. A short distance on the right is the Queen Elizabeth public house, rebuilt in 1928 on the site of an earlier pub. The mock-Tudor pub has now been demolished, together with other buildings in the street, to be replaced by a hotel and apartments.

Severn's on Middle Pavement in 1964, the last surviving fifteenth-century building in the city.
The building was acquired in 1900 by Severn's, who owned a wine and spirit business and restaurant in
the adjoining Georgian building. In 1956 the restaurant was extended to the timber-framed building, but
the venture was to last for only twelve more years before it closed when threatened by the building of the
Broad Marsh Centre. The outcry against the destruction of the old building saved this structure, although
the Georgian house was demolished (see page 51).

Severn's, Middle Pavement, being dismantled in 1969 before its removal to Castle Road where it was re-erected. A number of caves were discovered under the building – part of a series in the area. Unfortunately, when rebuilt, the old house was almost unrecognisable from the original (see page 51).

Low and Middle Pavements in 1967. These varied buildings range in age from the fifteenth-century Severn's and the Georgian Vault Hall in the foreground, to the Edwardian Postern Chambers at the corner of Drury Hill. These buildings, together with Willoughby House and the Assembly Rooms, made this area the finest architectural group in the city. Postern Chambers replaced the Postern Gate Inn where the gates to the town were locked each evening. When the Broad Marsh Centre was built the character of Middle Hill changed irrevocably.

Boots at 22 Goose Gate in 1963. This street is where the Boots empire began in 1849, when Jesse's father, John Boot, opened a herbal shop higher up Goose Gate. After the early death of John Boot, his widow Mary and the young Jesse continued the business with such success that, in 1881, Jesse, now in full control, began building new premises at 16–20 Goose Gate. By buying in bulk and using his promotional skills, Jesse was able to expand his company, opening new shops throughout the north of England.

Opposite below: The George Hotel in 1965 when it was owned by the Duke of Rutland. This is the oldest hotel in the city, having opened in 1822 as the George IV, and where Charles Dickens stayed when he appeared in Nottingham. Beyond the hotel are some of the bargain shops for which Hockley was noted.

Hockley in 1969 before Coalpit Lane was widened and renamed Cranbrook Street, with the consequent demolition of several of these shops. The old Maypole shop still remains with its tiled entrance. Ashmores, with its bargain arcade, has disappeared, but Hockley Church where John Wesley preached has been saved to be converted into apartments.

Above: Hockley in 1960 when there were no parking restrictions. On the left are two of the numerous clothiers of the district; Harrisons and Prossers, with the noted butchers – Seymours – in the same row. In the distance are Pullman's drapers, where customers' cash was shot in canisters along wire to a cashier, with the change and receipt returning in a similar way.

Excavating the old town wall in Hockley in 1970 before the construction of Cranbrook Street. As well as artefacts, numerous human bones were discovered. In the background is Woolworth's store which, when it opened in the 1930s, was a 3*d* and 6*d* shop – for example, a twenty-one-piece tea set was sold as individual items.

7

ST ANN'S AND SNEINTON

The Coachmaker's Arms at the corner of St Ann's Well Road and Union Road in 1968 when the majority of the district was threatened with demolition. The landlord of the pub was Adam Adams, which perhaps showed a lack of imagination by his parents.

Huntingdon Street Bus Station in 1968. As well as buses to the city's suburbs, coaches would leave here for the holiday resorts of the east and west coasts. This was a time when holidays abroad were becoming popular and Trent and Bartons were among the companies promoting continental destinations.

Passengers queuing at the Huntingdon Street Bus Station on a dismal day in 1964. These are unlikely to be holidaymakers – the destinations of the buses are Darlington, Newcastle and South Shields. The bus station was to remain until 1972 when the services were transferred to Mount Street and Broad Marsh.

Above: The Empress Bingo Casino, St Ann's Well Road, 1968. This started life as the New Empress Cinema, opening in 1928 and closing in 1960, unable to compete with the rival attraction of television. The New Empress was demolished during the clearance of St Ann's.

The Victoria Bingo Casino, St Ann's Well Road, 1968. Owned by Mecca, who also ran the nearby Empress Bingo, this was originally the Victoria Ballroom, one of the premier halls of the city. At one time the hall was known as the Power House, for it was then owned by the Electricity Board. In the 1930s the regular band was called the Commanders, led by the locally born Billy Merrin, and post-war Al Washbrooke's band became the resident orchestra.

Anti-war protesters marching along St Ann's Well Road in 1964. Intense feeling against the Vietnam War resulted in demonstrations such as this, with two of the marchers carrying a coffin. This march was peaceful under the watchful eye of a solitary policeman at the rear. In the background is the St Ann's Well Road Congregational Church which was to be pulled down with the remainder of these buildings in the early 1970s.

St Ann's Church at the corner of Coppice Road and St Ann's Well Road in 1968, when the district was a close-knit community revolving around the churches, clubs and public houses.

The Westminster Abbey Hotel at the junction of St Ann's Well Road and Ransom Road in 1970. Originally known as the Abbey, after its demolition a new public house named the Westminster was opened nearby in 1971. Within a year the pub's name was inexplicably changed to the Wheeltappers.

Below: The Admiral Dundas, St Ann's Well Road, 1969. On the right is the traditionally built Barclay's Bank and in the distance is the Westminster Bank, designed by Watson Fothergill. All these buildings were to be pulled down to the area's great loss.

Above: One of the backyards of St Ann's in 1972. These Victorian houses were among the worst in the city, without indoor toilets and having a communal yard. Unfortunately, the friendliness which existed in these close communities largely disappeared when the new St Ann's was built.

Lammas Lodge, also known as St Michael's Police Lodge, Huntingdon Street, in 1970. Built in 1860 in St Michael's Recreation Ground, the lodge also possessed a water fountain. After its demolition in 1975 the bells and Borough Arms from the building were removed to the Brewhouse Yard Museum.

Robin Hood Chase in 1970. This tree-lined avenue was created in the nineteenth century with substantial houses on each side. The avenue continues beyond Woodborough Road as Corporation Oaks and Elm Avenue then, with a break at Mansfield Road, the route continues through the Arboretum and the General Cemetery to Canning Circus. Unfortunately, the Chase has been truncated and many of the houses have been demolished.

A passer-by checking the forthcoming attractions at the Cavendish Cinema in 1961. The film being promoted is *The Wind of Change* starring Donald Pleasance. The cinema opened in 1938 and was an immediate success, particularly with youngsters at Saturday matinées. The popularity of television in the 1960s affected the Cavendish audiences, as with most cinemas, and it was forced to close in 1969. For a while the Cavendish became a bingo hall and when that failed the building was converted into a supermarket.

The Fox and Grapes, Southwell Road, in 1971. Known locally as 'Pretty Windows' from its decorative window panes, it was notorious for the unsolved murder of its landlord, George Wilson, on his doorstep in 1963. When the Wholesale Fruit and Vegetable Market opened in 1938, the public house was given a licence to open in the early hours of the morning for the benefit of the traders and customers. The pub changed its name to Peggers in 1986, but is now closed with its future uncertain.

The Nottingham Castle, Lower Parliament Street, in 1962. The public house is unaccountably named, situated without a view of its namesake. A well-built pub, the building was shortly to be pulled down and rebuilt on an adjoining plot – and renamed the Castle.

Above: The two remaining houses in Notintone Place in 1968 after the remainder had been demolished. The house on the right was the birthplace in 1829 of William Booth, the founder of the Salvation Army. After restoration, the house was refurnished in Victorian style with the adjoining house being opened as a museum. At the same time, an Eventide Home and Goodwill Centre was built nearby, opened in 1971 by Commissioner Catherine Bramwell-Booth, granddaughter of the founder of the Army.

The shell of Sneinton Windmill in 1970. Known as Green's Mill, the structure was gutted by fire in 1947 when it was being used as a furniture polish factory. The mill is named after George Green who lived here in the early nineteenth century. While studying at Caius College, Cambridge, he formulated the mathematical theories for which he became famous after his death. In 1974 a trust was established to restore the old mill as a memorial to the great Sneinton mathematician.

Sneinton Market in 1968 when it was still thriving. On the left is a second-hand shop selling anything from books to clothes and household goods. In recent years the market has suffered a decline and its future is unclear. The Victoria Baths in the background, now a leisure centre is also being threatened with closure.

Below: St Philip's Church, Pennyfoot Street, in 1960. The church was built in 1879 in memory of Thomas Adams, the lace manufacturer. After the church was closed in 1961, Boots demolished the building and constructed a research block here to complement the one in the background.

8

THE MEADOWS TO THE RIVER TRENT

Pleasure boats at the landing stages on the River Trent in 1968. Trevithick's and Brookhouse had been running river cruises and hiring out rowing boats for many years. In the background is the Bridgford Hotel, built in 1964 on the site of the Plaza Cinema, and later to become the Rushcliffe Centre.

Boots Head Office, Station Street, in 1964. The building was originally Hine & Mundella's hosiery factory, and was taken over by Jesse Boot in 1912. Beyond are the Boots printing works, built in 1950 after the earlier building was burnt down in the Blitz of 1941. After Boots transferred their head office to Beeston in 1968, this site was used as a car park until, in 2002, Capitol One built Loxley House here.

Below: Boots offices in Trent Street in 1964. The premises were bought from A.R. Atkey, motor engineer, at the beginning of the twentieth century and continued to be used until 1968.

The Burton Homes on London Road in 1971. These were founded in the nineteenth century by Ann Burton of Spaniel Row for twenty-four unmarried people over sixty years of age. They each received 15s per month and a supply of coal yearly. When the Meadows was redeveloped in the 1970s, these homes were pulled down and the residents moved to a new complex.

The Globe cinema at Trent Bridge in 1962. Built in 1914, in its early years the cinema was very successful, drawing audiences from West Bridgford where a cinema was not opened until 1931. After closing as a cinema in 1961, the Globe flirted with bingo for a short period before finally closing in 1962. On the right is Turney Brothers' leather works which was built in 1911–13, and continued in production until 1981 when the factory was converted into luxury apartments.

Shops on Arkwright Street in 1973, shortly before they were closed to be demolished. The street leading from the Midland Railway Station to Trent Bridge was the main shopping thoroughfare of the Meadows, fulfilling almost all the needs of the local residents. After the rebuilding of the district, St Saviour's Church remained but Arkwright Street was truncated and lost its importance.

The Nottingham Co-operative Society Mini Market on Arkwright Street in 1976, due to close following fire damage. Posters in the window advertise sliced loaves at 12½p, ½lb packs of butter at 19½p each and washing powder at 31p.

A row of boarded-up shops on Arkwright Street in 1973. Demolition was indiscriminate in the area. Following the clearance, a shopping precinct was opened in the centre of the new Meadows, but this was a poor substitute for the diverse shops on Arkwright Street.

A row of shops and houses on Arkwright Street in 1976, still standing in the midst of a wasteland, before they too were knocked down. In the background, visible through the smoke, are the Burton Homes, awaiting their turn to be demolished.

The fire in the main stand of the Nottingham Forest football ground on 24 August 1968, during a match between Forest and Leeds United. It was shortly before half-time when smoke began to filter through the stand and flames appeared. The referee, seeing the danger, abandoned the match and led the players off the field. The crowd, meanwhile, were moved in an orderly manner onto the pitch. By this time flames were sweeping through the main stand and spreading to the Trent End stand. The players were in danger beneath the main stand, but managed to escape unhurt.

Opposite below: The fire at the City Ground from across the River Trent. Spectators are streaming away from the ground which is covered in smoke. The Nottingham Forest chairman, Tony Wood, pledged the stand would be rebuilt – in the meantime the team played their next six games at the Meadow Lane ground without winning a match.

Police Constable Michael Pickford on horseback controlling the crowd which spilled onto the pitch at the City Ground, when fire raced through the main stand during the match in August 1968. Fortunately, there were no injuries to the crowd of over 30,000, but many of Forest's records, trophies and memorabilia were lost in the blaze.

Tony Woodcock and John Robertson celebrating, after Nottingham Forest had won the European Cup by beating Malmo 1-0 in Munich in 1979. It was an extraordinary achievement for an unfancied team, having already overcome Liverpool, A.E.K. Athens, Grasshoppers Zurich and Cologne on their way to the final.

The huge crowd of Nottingham Forest supporters waiting outside the County Hall in 1979 for the arrival of their team with the European Cup. The team had already made a victory tour around the city on an open-top bus and an appearance on the balcony of the Council House. Nottingham Forest had defied all expectations in winning the trophy and were to repeat the feat the following season – beating Hamburg 1-0 in Madrid.

Opposite above: The Nottingham Forest chairman Stuart Dryden shaking Brian Clough's hand on Clough's appointment as manager in January 1975. Forest had been relegated to the Second Division of the Football League in 1972 and a 2-0 home defeat by Notts. County in the local Derby in December 1974 was the last straw, and Forest fans urged the club to make Clough the manager.

The Nottingham Canal in 1970, when it was in decline as a working waterway. The days when 30-ton barges from Hull would tie up at the British Waterways warehouse were gone and the building was becoming derelict. In the 1980s new life was brought into the area when one of the old buildings was converted into a canal museum and the Fellows, Morton & Clayton warehouse was turned into a pub, brewing and selling real ale. In the 1990s the British Waterways warehouse was converted into a number of bars and a footbridge was built across the canal. At the same time, the new Magistrates' Courts were constructed on the south bank of the canal.

The men's urinal on the London Road stretch of the Nottingham Canal in 1968. This cast iron structure, made by the Bridgnorth Iron Foundry, was one of the last nineteenth-century urinals still in Nottingham at that time. After its removal, it was taken to the Nottingham Industrial Museum in Wollaton Park.

9

LENTON AND WOLLATON

The erection of the Willoughby Street flats in 1966. After the demolition of the old houses in the district, these brilliantly white tower blocks were built on the site. Unlike the Hyson Green flats built in the 1970s, these buildings have survived and become accepted by the tenants.

Queen Elizabeth II touring the Raleigh Cycle Company works with Chairman Leslie L. Roberts in 1968. Here, the Queen is being shown RSW Mk II bicycles, which were one of the company's great successes of the 1960s. The visit lasted over an hour, with the Queen being driven through the works in a specially adapted Land Rover. After the tour the Queen was driven to the Council House for a reception, passing thousands of children who were unfortunately drenched by a sudden downpour of rain.

An assembly room at Raleigh in 1960, the year in which the company merged with the British Cycle Company – part of Tube Investments. Raleigh then took over the management of both companies and began producing a number of classic cycles.

Striking workers at Raleigh in 1964. This was the decade when industrial relations became strained throughout the country. The dispute arose over redundancies in the works and was the longest post-war strike in Nottingham. By the end of the strike, more than 2,000 workers had been laid off. Raleigh were to continue manufacturing bicycles until 1999 but, with the increasing competition from Far Eastern countries, the company began importing cheaper cycles from abroad.

The small shop at the corner of Gregory Street and Abbey Street in 1966, where the Nottingham Co-operative movement began. The shop was opened in 1863 by the Lenton Industrial and Provident Society, and was so successful that a second shop was opened in Lenton and further expansion took place in other suburbs. In 1873 the title of the business changed to the Lenton and Nottingham Co-operative Society, and in 1906 the company was renamed the Nottingham Co-operative Society.

The Lenton Methodist Church, Castle Boulevard, in 1970 – known locally as the Tin Chapel. After its closure at the beginning of the twentieth century, the building was first occupied by Crampton Organs and in 1921 by Clement Pianos. The company were to remain here until 1980, the building surviving until 2002.

The Butt Houses on Derby Road in 1968. These were estate houses built in the early nineteenth century by the local landowning family, the Gregorys. While not great architecturally, the row of houses was pleasing in its garden setting. Despite having a preservation order on the houses, in 1975 the decision was made to demolish the properties and build twelve maisonettes on the site.

The Nazareth House, Abbey Street, in 1978. The Congregation of the Poor Sisters of Nazareth moved to Lenton in 1881 from premises in Cranmer Street. During the following century the Sisters cared for almost 4,000 adults and children. In the 1990s, with more exacting requirements being imposed on care homes, the decision was taken to close Nazareth House. On 16 June 2002 a farewell Mass of Thanksgiving was held at the house which, after demolition, was replaced by a group of town houses.

Hicking & Pentecost, Castle Boulevard, in 1972. The dyeing and bleaching company was founded in Station Street in 1871, moving here shortly afterwards. The building and its 165ft chimney were demolished in 1978, ending over a century of the dyeing industry here. The site has now been used for housing.

The Albion Inn, Sherwin Road, in 1970. Converted from a private house, the Kimberley Brewery public house has a Sheltie keeping a watchful eye from the roof of the bay window. The pub survived the demolition of the surrounding houses for ten years, being pulled down in 1980.

A wintry scene in Wollaton Park in 1969. The freezing February of that year made the slope in front of the hall ideal for sledging.

Police Constable Paul Cooper on Loxley in Wollaton Park in 1974, when the mounted section of the city police was based in the stables of the hall. Budget pressures are today putting the city's mounted police under threat, but eight horses and six officers have been spared by a deal struck with a local company to supply free hay. The mounted police are invaluable in Nottingham, attending football matches, demonstrations, the Lord Mayor's Parade and being a reassuring presence in the city.

Teddy boys and girls dancing at the Cocked Hat, Broxtowe Lane, in 1960. The boys are wearing drape jackets, drainpipe trousers, crêpe-soled shoes and have Brylcreemed hair with a quiff; the girls are wearing circular skirts and have their hair in a ponytail. With or without a partner, enjoyment was to be had shaking and swirling to the music.

10

RADFORD
NORTHWARDS

Radford Road in 1966 – the main shopping thoroughfare of Radford. On the left, boasting a public clock, is Staddon's, with Beach's Stores – the two largest shops in Radford. Before shopping centres changed people's buying habits, the shops in this street could supply almost every need.

Player's No.2 factory, Radford Road, in 1972 – the year the Horizon factory opened in Lenton. The factory was designed by Player's architects and opened in 1932 with the latest automated machinery. The 1930s was the period when working at Player's, with their annual bonus, was the ambition of many of the workers in Nottingham. By the 1970s, with concerns over the danger of smoking increasing, Player's were beginning to diversify. This factory and the others in Radford were gradually phased out and the building was then demolished. With foresight, this notable structure would have been saved to be redeveloped as an apartment block.

Below: Workers at Player's in 1960 constructing wooden packing cases. Besides producing cigarettes and loose tobacco, the firm also manufactured their own cartons, many bearing the famous Nottingham Castle trademark.

Employees at the Cellular Clothing Company, Vernon Road, 1961. This was the cutting-out room of the factory which produced shirts and underwear for both the home and export markets. One of the many such factories in the city at the time, almost all were eventually to close down, unable to compete with manufacturers in the Far East.

A white Shipstone's shire-horse pulling a small dray, loaded with barrels of beer, along Radford Road in 1968. This was a familiar sight in those days, particularly in Radford near the Star Brewery. In the background is Joselyn's scooter shop – when these machines were being promoted in this country. The more uncertain and cooler weather conditions here made scooters less popular in Britain than on the continent.

Lenos Cinema, Radford Road, in 1968. The films being shown are *A Challenge for Robin Hood* and *Ringo and his Golden Pistol*, the final presentation before its closure. The cinema opened as the Little John Picture Palace in 1911, but after a change of ownership in 1912, the cinema was renamed Lenos Royal Picturedrome as a tribute to Dan Leno, the famous pantomime dame. After closing as a cinema, a bingo hall was opened here, and finally the building was used as a retail warehouse. After demolition, a housing complex was built on the site.

The Boulevard Bingo Club, previously the Boulevard Cinema, in 1960. The cinema opened in 1910, but dwindling audiences forced its closure in 1956 and it became one of the first bingo halls in the city.

The Capitol Cinema, Aifreton Road, in 1968, the year the cinema closed and was converted into a bingo hall. The advertised attractions are *Hercules Attacks* starring Gordon Scott, and *The Shadow of Zorro* with Frank Latimore – both films instantly forgettable. The cinema opened in 1936, immediately attracting audiences away from the old converted cinemas in the surrounding area. The building has now been granted Grade II listed status and converted into the Mount Zion Millennium Church.

The Vernon Picture House, Vernon Road, in 1967, when it had already become a bingo hall. The cinema opened in 1917 when the admission prices were 3*d*, 4*d* and 6*d*. The building occupied an awkward corner plot, and when Cinemascope was installed the image shrank to a letter-box slit on the screen.

Denman Street in 1964, then still a street of small independent shops serving the needs of the local community. When this area was cleared in the 1960s, high-rise flats and townhouses were built here for the dispossessed residents.

Old Peveril or Debtors' Prison, St Peter's Street, in 1968, awaiting demolition. This eighteenth-century building was originally the Radford Workhouse which closed in 1838. In 1842 Peveril Prison, which had previously been situated behind the White Hart at Lenton, was transferred here. Peveril Prison was the building where debtors found guilty by the Court of the Honour of Peveril were confined. The court was instituted in 1113 by William Peveril and was finally abolished by an Act of Parliament in 1849. After the closure of the prison this building was converted into two houses.

Lumley Castle public house, Radford Road, in 1961, one of the many Victorian pubs which were pulled down in the inner suburbs in the 1970s. This is now the site of a supermarket car park, passed by Nottingham's new trams.

Floods in Nuthall Road in 1963 when the River Leen overflowed its banks, giving these children an unusual cycling experience. Since then, flood defence work has made this scene unlikely in the future.

Children playing in Arnot Hill Park in 1961. Summer holidays then would bring youngsters to parks like this, especially if the weather was warm, to play at the water's edge, perhaps to fish for minnows or to paddle. This was a carefree time when children had a freedom denied to today's generation of youngsters.

Sunbathers at Bulwell Lido in 1966. One of three lidos in Nottingham, this facility opened in 1937 and was immediately very popular. Although apparently a hot day, there do not appear to be many swimmers in the pool. The lido closed in 2003, a victim of falling attendances and council cutbacks.

North Place, Old Basford, in 1965. These nineteenth-century cottages were scheduled for demolition, the inhabitants being moved into new high-rise flats in the vicinity. These old properties had only the minimum of facilities but the new accommodation proved only marginally better, being poorly constructed and demolished within fifteen years of their erection.

David Lane, Old Basford, in 1965. These small stone dwellings were built for workers in the lace and hosiery trades, which were rapidly growing industries in the early nineteenth century.

11

GOOSE FAIR

Goose Fair from the Forest in 1970. In this view only the helter-skelter, renamed the Cresta Run, and the Retro-Ride, a version of the rotor, appear above the favourite rides, such as the horses and the dodgems.

The opening ceremony of the Goose Fair in 1967. After the proclamation by the town clerk, the Lord Mayor, Councillor Arthur Roberts, declares the fair open – the bells are rung, the roundabouts begin to turn and the music adds to the excitement.

The Lord Mayor and Lady Mayoress, Councillor and Mrs Arthur Roberts, entering the Goose Fair in 1967 with, behind them, Chief Constable Thomas Moore and Town Clerk Philip Vine. Opening the Goose Fair is one of the fixtures in the Mayoral calendar, and although the fair now starts on the first Wednesday in October, the opening ceremony still takes place at noon the following day.

The Lord Mayor, Councillor Arthur Roberts, on a scooter, unsure how a man with such a great office has come to be in this situation. The Sheriff, Henry Bryan, and the Lady Mayoress, Mrs Arthur Roberts, are evidently enjoying themselves.

The Sheriff and his Lady emerging from the tunnel in the ghost train. After rides on a number of roundabouts, the civic party try their luck at the shooting range and the coconut shy, invariably winning prizes before returning to the Council House for a civic lunch.

Gipsies in their booths in front gardens of Mount Hooton Road in 1968. Fortune-tellers were no longer allowed on the Goose Fair site, but several exhorted passers-by in nearby streets to have their palms read. Gipsy Lee, on the left, claimed to be the Royal Gipsy, while Laura Boswell asserted she was consulted by royalty on Epsom Downs.

Above: A cowboy and cowgirl endeavouring
to attract an audience to their Wild West Show
in 1960. This type of show, with its sharp
shooting, knife-throwing and rope tricks, is no
longer seen at the fair. State-of-the-art riding
machines now predominate.

Opposite above: The crowded entrance to the
Goose Fair from Gregory Boulevard in 1960.
The old-fashioned rides, such as the Waltzer
and Galloping Horses, still predominate, but for
the more adventurous there are the Meteorite
and the Skid. There was still an avenue of side
shows, including a boxing booth and a wild west
show.

Youngsters having their age guessed by an
itinerant dressed as a cowboy in 1967. The
charge was 6*d* and a lucky charm was the prize
if he was incorrect.

Above: Billy Hood's Boxing Booth at the Goose Fair in 1966. Once one of the staple entertainments at the fair, this show, as with the adjoining Voodoo Girl, is now out of fashion. Local men would be encouraged to box one of the booth's professionals – to be awarded £5 if they survived three rounds.

Two young girls eating toffee apples at the Goose Fair in 1961. These were one of the treats at the fair, although beneath the coating of toffee a cooking apple could lurk.

Two youngsters with candyfloss at the fair in 1967. This was another staple of the fair, along with hot dogs, Grantham Ginger Bread, mushy peas and brandy-snap. The girl on the left appears to have had a lucky win at one of the prize stalls.

Below: The Moon Rocket at the fair in 1970. This was then a death-defying ride, but rather tame when compared to the machines of the twenty-first century.

A vendor dressed in a top hat and tail coat at the Goose Fair in 1968, with his entire stock in a small suitcase. He appears to be enjoying a quiet drink and a cigarette while awaiting customers for 'Gloworm', which claims to be 'Mystifying, amusing and amazing'.

Below: Young people on the Waltzer in 1964. The girl in the centre is apparently too scared to look, but her companions are not at all concerned. The dizziness comes after the ride with the first few steps on the ground.